MW00438117

Coffee with God:

A 40-Day Poetry Devotional

by

Jean Mikulski

DORRANCE
PUBLISHING CO
EST. 1920
PITTSBURGH, PENNSYLVANIA 15238

Dorrance Publishing Co
585 Alpha Drive
Suite 103
Pittsburgh, PA 15238
Visit our website at www.dorrancebookstore.com

ISBN: 978-1-6376-4109-5
eISBN: 978-1-6376-4946-6

This poetry devotional is dedicated to my Lord and Savior, with whom I have a daily cup of coffee. I would also like to thank my family and friends who encouraged me throughout this journey. I love you and thank you for support.

Coffee with God

JOHN 14:16, 17

[16]And I will ask the Father, and he will give you another Counselor to be with you forever—[17]the Spirit of truth.

The world cannot accept him, because it neither sees him nor knows him. But, you know him, for he lives with you and will be in you.

COFFEE WITH GOD

In the newness of the morning
It's your face I long to see
Will you sit for just a moment...
Have a cup of coffee with me?

I love you, oh so dearly
And enjoy this time with you
Let's talk and chat a while
My heart longs for words so true

Faithful, ever faithful
No other can I trust
I yearn for what you'll whisper
The Holy Spirit's words a must

My earthly father gave such love
So precious and so dear
But now I understand in full
That God deserves my fear

Reverence and worship
Praise and thanks are due
For no one ever will compare
With God, whose love is true

Our hearts need to turn

back to God and

feel Him ever near

He's our King, who deserves

revere

REVELATION 22:6-7, 12

The angel said to me, "These words are trustworthy and true.
The Lord, the God of the spirits of the prophets, sent his angel
to show his servants the things that must soon take place."
⁷"Behold, I am coming soon! Blessed is he who keeps the words
of the prophecy in this book."

¹² "Behold, I am coming soon! My reward is with me, and
I will give to everyone according to what he has done."

YOUR CHOICE

Anger and confusion
Bitterness and strife
All have become
A constant part of life

Are we okay today
Tomorrow are we not?
The news that divides our thinking
All seems like a sinister plot

Will my job still be there
Will my bills keep piling up?
When will this rollercoaster
Of fear come to a stop?

This life matters; that life doesn't
When will all this end?
What's right is wrong; what's wrong is right
Such evil around each bend

Songs and prayers to God above
Are keenly becoming halted
What seems like innocent solutions
Are Satan's schemes to assault us

The time is drawing near, my friend
Open your eyes and look around
This is the time to call on God
While He can still be found

The plan in place since the world began
Is quickly beginning to unfold
Christ will return without doubt
As the Bible has foretold

Only those you have received
Christ Jesus as their Savior
Will be caught up with Him in the air
To reign with Him forever

Wake up and recognize
That God's Word is ever true
He gave these signs and warnings
The choice to believe is up to you

DEUTERONOMY 5:11

"You shall not misuse the name of the Lord your God, for the Lord will not hold anyone guiltless who misuses his name."

#OMG

Have we stooped to depths so low
As to hashtag God's own name?
A frivolous OMG
Diminishes God's acclaim

God watches from the heavens
As we mindlessly spell or say
"Oh My God!" or OMG
He's become a simple phrase

Instead of our Mighty King
He is lessened to three letters
"OMG... look at that!"
Is just a new trendsetter

Without a thought
Our mighty God
Shrinks to an easy tag
An everyday dynamic
Used as a social hashtag

Our hearts need to turn
Back to God
And feel Him ever near
Instead of just an OMG
He's our King, who deserves revere

Matthew 7:12

So in everything, do to others what you would have them do to you, for this sums up the Law and the Prophets.

Ephesians 4:31, 32

[31]*Get rid of all bitterness, rage and anger, brawling and slander, along with every form of malice.* [32]*Be kind and compassionate to one another, forgiving each other, just as in Christ GOD forgave you.*

THE "I" IN SIN

We live in such a different time
Our values are now jaded
"Do unto others as you would want"
Are principles that have faded

Social opinion that matters most
Is the one that "I" have stated
"I" don't care what you believe
Your stance is just outdated

How dare that you should disagree
Unhinged "I" will become
Don't try to voice another thought
"I'll" state, "You must be dumb!"

Then "I'll" post to "JUST BE KIND"
Because that's what "I" am
Unless our views become aligned
You cannot be my friend

All this banter seems to speak
To how far we've lost our way
The care for others ceases
When we remove GOD from our day

The world would be a better place
If we took a look within
And asked GOD for forgiveness
To stop this "I" in sin

ISAIAH 55:6, 7

Seek the LORD while he may be found; call on him while he is near. ⁷Let the wicked forsake his way and the evil man his thoughts. Let him turn to the LORD, and he will have mercy on him, and to our God, for he will freely pardon.

MATTHEW 24:42

⁴² "Therefore keep watch, because you do not know on what day your Lord will come."

WITHOUT WARNING

COVID came our way one dreadful day
And spread throughout our land
Folks faltered, feared and trembled
Was this sent from God's own hand?

Many spoke of things
How time stood still
Halted business; canceled plans
Life was curbed against our will

No more rushing here or bustling there
A deafening silence without end
It seemed strange and eerie at the time
No more functions to attend

It makes me think of a time to come
When Jesus will return
Taking those who longingly waited
Kept the faith; now this they earned

It will be strange and frightening
One taken while the other remains
All happening in the blink of an eye
Such anguish and cries in vain

So now is the time to seek the Lord
While He can still be found
And you will also be ready
When the great trumpet will sound

HABAKKUK 1:2-4, 2:3

How long, O Lord, must I call for help, but you do not listen? Or cry out to you, "Violence!" but you do not save?

³Why do you make me look at injustice? Why do you tolerate wrong? Destruction and violence are before me; there is strife, and conflict abounds;

⁴Therefore the law is paralyzed, and justice never prevails. The wicked hem in the righteous, so that justice is perverted.

²:³For the revelation awaits an appointed time; it speaks of the end and will not prove false. Though it linger, wait for it; it will certainly come and will not delay.

GOD SEEMS SILENT

Our prayers are sent to heaven
Each and every day
How long will You be silent
And seem to turn away

We cry out for justice
Why do you tolerate the wrong?
Destruction and violence surround us
Conflict progresses in throngs

The law seems paralyzed
Justice never prevails
The wicked hem in the righteous
Peace and harmony seem to fail

O Lord, please shake the heavens
And set our hearts ablaze
Fill us with your Holy Spirit
Cause our mouths to sing your praise

Perform the awesome wonders
That your word says we can expect
May your name be renown throughout the earth
As the Mighty God who acts

You see the wrongs surrounding
Your silence is not at all true
You heard our cries for deliverance
The moment our prayers were lifted to you

LUKE 19:41-44

*As he approached Jerusalem and saw
the city, he wept over it* [42]*and said,
"If you, even you, had only known
on this day what would bring you
peace—but now it is hidden from
your eyes."*

JEREMIAH 17:7

[7]*But blessed is the man who trusts
in the Lord, whose confidence
is in him.*

TURN WHOLEHEARTEDLY

O Jesus, how you must weep
When you see our cities and towns
The destruction, strife and hatred
The sins and evils know no bounds

Peace is now hidden from our eyes
Enemies circle to destroy
The way of life found in you
Has become lost in great discord

Remove the "scales" that cloud our eyes
Open wide our hearts to see
That only true peace and forgiveness
Comes from you—because you died on that tree

God's house is a house of prayer
A holy refuge for times like these
But evil is trying to shut the doors
From fulfilling our Godly needs

We urgently seek for answers
Divinely revealed in miraculous ways
For our hope is solely found in You, Lord
When we take the time to pray

Lord God, you alone are our refuge
Our strength in times of distress
We must put our trust in You alone
To live our lives fully blessed

Save us, Lord, and we will be saved
Heal us so that healed we will be
Let these words of God be fulfilled
When we turn to You wholeheartedly

MATTHEW 24:31, 33-35

[31]And he will send his angels with a loud trumpet call, and they will gather his elect from the four winds, from one end of the heavens to the other. [33]Even so, when you see all these things, you know that it is near, right at the door. [34]I tell you the truth, this generation will certainly not pass away until all these things have happened. [35]Heaven and earth will pass away, but my words will never pass away."

TAKE HEED

The prophets of old
Distinctly foretold
Of events and happenings to come

Warnings and signs
Visions from the divine
God-given to open man's eyes

Clearly God yearns
For man to turn
And acknowledge Him alone

How long must He endure
Those who ignore
All passages divinely written

He's been patient and kind
Giving us time
To ask to be forgiven

Though ages ago
Still this we know
These forewarning will come to fruition

God's Son will return
For those unturned
By the world's standards and evils

Be wise and take heed
It's God that we need
In the end, that's all that will matter

2 TIMOTHY 4:3,4

*For the time will come when men will
not put up with sound doctrine. Instead,
to suit their own desires, they will gather
around them a great number of teachers
to say what their itching ears want to hear.
4They will turn their ears away from the
truth and turn aside to myths.*

IN GOD WE STILL MUST TRUST

Our great nation was based on
"In God We Trust"
The constitution, the pledge to our flag
Were written with God as our focus

Our heartstrings are now pulled by earthly pleasures
The chords once strong are now strained
The endeavors to pursue our desires
Have made God no longer attained

Where is the Lord in all of this
As we drift farther away
His principles and commands no longer come to our minds
As they did in our grandparents' day

We have changed our perspectives
And totally lost our way
Our sought-after idols of self-indulgence
Are clearly leading us astray

God's more than a name to frivolously mention
Our trust in Him is to remain
He's still the same as years gone by
And tomorrow He'll be the same

Wake up and return to the one true God
For only then will we see
The redemption and healing; His plan for all
That He offers unconditionally

I TIMOTHY 1:17

Now to the King eternal, immortal, invisible,
the only God, be honor and glory for ever and ever, Amen.

GOD IS STILL ON THE THRONE

The world is frenzied; hope seems lost
Our focus is on man, not God
No matter the outcome of this moment in time
God is still on the throne

From Biblical days to our current time
Wars and strife have always existed
Chaos and fear have taken hold
Yet, God is still on the throne

Man's wants and desires
Are all that matter
In this world now shrouded in darkness
Right is now wrong; wrong is now right
But God is still on the throne

Quite clearly the answer to all these problems
Can be found if we turn back to God
He'll forgive our sins and heal our land
For God is still on the throne

God gave us a spirit of power; not fear
Of love and self-control
So be watchful and strong; stand firm in the faith
Our God is still on the throne

All things work together for God's purpose
He alone rules this world He designed
May His will be done on earth as in heaven
For our God is still on the throne!

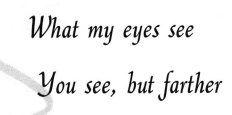

What my eyes see

You see, but farther

ISAIAH 57:15, 18

For this is what the high and lofty One says—
He who lives forever, whose name is holy:
"I live in a high and holy place, but also with him who is contrite and
lowly in spirit, to revive the heart of the contrite."

[18]I have seen his ways, but I will heal him: I will guide him and restore
comfort to him.

CHAPTERS OF MY LIFE

Broken spirit and in pain
I can't seem to understand
Each day I wake and wonder
Is this really God's main plan?

Remembering Job from Bible days
Who was tested and certainly tried
I know I'll need his kind of faith
To walk closely by Your side

Open my heart to keep your ways
Be steadfast and not turn weary
Of learning, praying, growing strong
To guide me through this journey

And when the chapters of my life
Are complete and sealed in glory
May it reflect a faithful soul
Rewarded for her story

MATTHEW 14:27-31

[27]But Jesus immediately said to them:
"Take courage! It is I. Don't be afraid."
[28]"Lord, if it's you," Peter replied, "tell me
To come to you on the water."
[29]"Come," he said
Then Peter got down out of the boat,
walked on the water and came toward
Jesus. [30]But when he saw the wind, he was afraid and,
beginning to sink, cried out, "Lord, save me!"
[31]Immediately Jesus reached out his hand and
caught him. "You of little faith," he said, "why
did you doubt?"

HELP ME KEEP MY EYES UPON YOU

When I'm troubled about tomorrow
And face problems I don't understand
Help me keeps my eyes upon You
As I reach out for your hand

When waves of fear surround me
And no end seems in sight
Help me keep my eyes upon You
As You whisper, "Hold on tight"

When situations drown my soul
And I'm sinking in despair
Help me keep my eyes upon You
For I know you always care

When happiness and joy
Are found throughout my day
Help me keep my eyes upon You
And remember to give you praise

Whatever the circumstance
I must face in my earthly plan
Help me keep my eyes upon You
For You alone hold my hand

PSALM 33:18

But the eyes of the LORD are on those who fear him,
on those whose hope is in his unfailing love

GOD SEES

What my eyes see, oh God
You see, but farther
Guide me where you'd have me go
For you are my Father

Ups and downs, stumbles and falls
You lead me ever
Lifting me to higher ground
Piecing me together

Meant for me, these trials and errors
To teach "Your will be done"
Pressing me on to look to thee
For this race I run

When my earthly life shall end
And I stand before you
May you say, "Well done, my child"
I saw what you could do

MATTHEW 6:33

But seek first his kingdom and his righteousness, and all these things will be given to you as well.

IF TO WHEN

If I rested upon Your word
And not words that fill my head
The joy and peace that could be found
Would fill my soul instead

If I went straight to Your word
Without discussion with a friend
I'd find the answer sooner
Then wallowing without end

If I prayed in earnest
Laying my burdens at Your feet
Instead of carrying them alone
My needs You would willingly meet

May I opt to turn my "ifs"
Into daily times of "when"
For only "when" I choose You first
Will Your best for me begin

ZEPHANIAH 3:17

The Lord your God is with you,
he is mighty to save. He will
take great delight in you, he
will quiet you with his love,
he will rejoice over you
with singing.

RENEW MY SPIRIT

The sounds of the world around you
Deafen the voice of God
The everyday distractions
Hush His words of love

Tuning in to listen closely
Takes more time then we allow
Our heads are filled with "what comes next"
Instead of "STOP" for just awhile

Devotions read without deep thought
Only fill a daily practice
Getting it done so the routine is fulfilled
In the end, just proves worthless

It requires discipline to take the time
To breathe in and settle down
Allow the Holy Spirit to visit;
Feel His presence all around

He will quiet you with His love
As He delights in His time with you
He'll rejoice over you with singing
As your spirit He renews

PSALM 56:8

Record my lament;
list my tears on your scroll—
are they not in your record?

BOTTLED TEARS

My tears are stored in a bottle
Reserved only for me
My Heavenly Father has a record of them
In a book for His eyes to see

As they are shed before Him
In earnest prayer raised to His throne
Each drop represents
A request from my soul alone

My heart cries out to you
With longing and with passion
For your Word clearly states
You can do far more than I even imagine

Sweet, loving Father
Please open that bottle of mine
If only to dry one tear at a time
I'll accept your will divine

So, as I trust You with my tears
Be merciful, I pray
For I long for the day
When ALL tears will be wiped away

When God's words are spo-

ken

On them you can rely

Jeremiah 29:11-14

MY PLANS FOR YOU

For I know the plans I have for you
Declares the Lord above
Plans of hope and a future
Sent to you with love

When you call upon my name
I will be ever true
With all your heart you seek me
I will be found by you

I will draw you back
From sin that made you roam
I'll restore what you have lost
And gather you safely home

My promises are always kept
For I never lie
When my words are spoken
Upon them you can rely

MATTHEW 5:3-12

BEAUTIFUL BEATITUDES

Be satisfied with what you have
For the Kingdom of Heaven is yours
Comfort those who have suffered loss
It's a blessing for those who mourn
Be gentle in handling others
For the earth will be given to you
If you hunger and thirst for righteousness
God will fill your heart anew
Strive to be merciful
For mercy, to you, will return
Keep your heart pure from sin
Together, with you, God yearns
Be the one to pursue peace
For God's child you will become
Suffering for your beliefs
Because it offends someone
Should only make your soul rejoice
And bring joy to your heart
For heaven is your reward
From God you will never part

PSALM 23

THE LORD'S PRAYER POEM

Our Father in heaven
Your name be praised
We await your kingdom to come
May we do the will that you purpose on earth
As in heaven your will is done
Daily supply the provisions we need
Forgive our wrongs, as we are to forgive other's misdeeds
Allow no temptations to lead us astray
And deliver us from Satan's evils each day

For all power, glory and honor are yours
Here on earth and in heaven

Amen

MATTHEW 7:1, 2

DON'T JUDGE

It's so easy to see the speck
In another person's eye
To point it out; talk about
And miss the board we deny

It's so easy to blame another's sickness or misfortune
On a sin they must have hidden
For surely that's what happens
When you commit something that is forbidden

Before you speak, phone or share
Stop and look within
Don't judge another's problem
And forget that you have sin

The Bible clearly tell us
To judge means judged we'll be
The measure we dole out
Will come back in the same degree

Before we point the finger
At wrongs that others do
Remember to show mercy
Just as Jesus has shown you

God's gift of

matchless wonders

Revelation 4:11

"You are worthy, our LORD and GOD, to receive glory and honor and power, for you created all things, and by your will they were created and have their being."

THE BEAUTY OF GOD'S MAJESTY

The beauty of *GOD's* majesty
I pause to view and see
The wonders of his handiwork
Displayed for you and me

Such splendor and magnificence
The grass, the trees, the hills
Declaring all *GOD's* glory
His spoken word fulfilled

The carpet of the earth
Thoughtfully laid with grass and soil
The lighting of the heavens
Set in place without hand or toil

The birds sing out their melody
Songs raised to *GOD's* own ears
Praising the creator
For provision without fears

Such a marvelous creation
Designed by the Master's plan
To bestow His awesome blessings
For all since the world began

JOB 12:7-10

[7] "But ask the animals, and they will teach you, or the birds of the air, and they will tell you; [8] or speak to the earth, and it will teach you, or let the fish of the sea inform you. [9] Which of all these does not know that the hand of the LORD has done this? [10] In his hand is the life of every creature and the breath of all mankind."

SUMMER PORCH

Sitting quietly
On my back porch swing
A glorious summer morning
Listening to the songbirds sing

A cup of coffee in hand
A time of peace; not care
A moment to drink in
God's presence everywhere

Sights and sounds surrounding
Like an orchestrated melody
The Master's fine tuning
Of the earth's designed beauty

A gentle breeze softly flows
And brings a cool reminder
That each breath I am given
Is a gift from my Designer

A picture-perfect moment
Awakening all my senses
God's gift of matchless wonders
Providentially commences

PSALM 42:8

By day the Lord directs his love,
At night his song is with me—
a prayer to the God of my life.

NIGHTTIME CHOIR

The stillness of early morning
Is such a sweet delight
Nighttime still holds its place
Awaiting dawn's new light

The sounds of nighttime singers
Soft, rich chirps that fill the air
Surround the dark with music
A soft ballad that they share

The beauty of their song
Rises in perfect harmony
An A Cappella choir
Rings out in melodious unity

What a wonderous awakening
To sounds ordinarily unheard
As we lie in slumber
A choir is performing undeterred

Their performance will conclude
When the sun lights the sky
The curtain will close
Until the next sunset draws nigh

PSALM 42:8

By day the Lord directs his love,
at night his song is with me—
a prayer to the God of my life.

THE WORLD AT ITS BEST

A peaceful summer morning
Not spoiled by daily cares
A wondrous moment of solace
Free from the world's affairs

A cool breeze softly blows
And sparks a harmonic tune
Played by a windchime
Singing to the moon

The darkness has yet to leave the sky
The birds still in their nest
So hard to tell this time goodbye
When the world is at its best

GENESIS 8:22

*"As long as the earth endures, seedtime
and harvest, cold and heat,
summer and winter, day and night
will never cease."*

TIME TO HARVEST

A chill has come to the air
The warmth of summer fades
The chirps that filled the summer night
Fall silent from their serenade

The sky is filled with twinkling lights
Dotting up the sky
The stillness of the crisp, cool night
Waves the summer sky goodbye

The season changes rapidly
How fast the summer flew
It's time to give the earth a rest
Until spring's fresh debut

The leaves change their color
Hues beautifully displayed
Before they fall to the ground
The act, each year, replayed

Fall actively takes its place
Her season to reign at hand
God's wonderous time of harvest
Designed by His perfect plan

I am given,

from above,

The amount God

meant for me

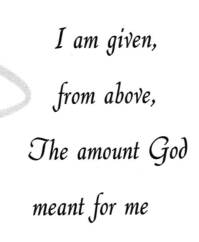

PHILIPPIANS 4:19

And my GOD will meet all your needs according to his glorious riches in Christ Jesus.

WISDOM FROM DOGS

Oh, the wisdom in the things
We stop to view in full
Though some may think it's nothing
God reveals to teach the soul

I watch as my dogs race to take
The bigger portion given
Not understanding the amount
Per size, was the right provision

Given in love, that perfect amount
Not meant to deprive or withhold
Becomes a battle to procure
The prize they think they're owed

It gives me pause to think that I
Do exactly as they do
I scramble to get the bigger things
That God says, "Not for you!"

May I take and learn from this
A lesson so clear to see
I am given from above
The amount God meant for me

LUKE 12:31

But seek his kingdom, and these things will
be given to you as well.

GOD'S TRUE PROVISION

I want this, give me that
Make my life complete
But did you take the time
To sit at the Savior's feet

Are you truly needy?
Or caught in a vicious snare
Of climbing, seeking, hoping
Never taking it to prayer

Are you one who labels
Your life as a Christian child
Yet daily lives without power
That comes when your head is bowed

God's never far from our cry
If we take the time to call
Leaving it up to His plan
To be our all in all

He'll meet your need
He'll answer your plea
Though it may not be the response
You requested and presented
When begging for your wants

Yet He knows without a doubt
What is want and what is need
If you trust and wait on Him
He'll reveal how to proceed

So, take the time to stop
To pray, obey and listen
And in God's timing
Your NEED will become provision

HEBREWS 6:1

Therefore let us leave the elementary teachings about Christ and go on to maturity, not laying again the foundation of repentance from acts that lead to death, and of faith in God

INFANT OR ADULT CHRISTIAN

Too many years I've allowed myself
To be an "infant" Christian
So many times, I could have been
Relying on God's provision

Instead I took the easy route
Of handling trials on my own
Never stopping and praying
Laying them at His throne

Self-reliance can be a snare
That entangles to the core
When a simple cry of "help"
Could have opened Heaven's door

It's time to put my faith in God
And leave my childish ways
Fully trust that God is by my side
And there He always stays

Rely on answers; not my own
Designed specifically
By my Heavenly Father
Who knows what's best for me

Psalm 84:11

*For the Lord God is a sun and shield; the Lord
bestows favor and honor; no good thing does
he withhold from those whose walk is blameless.*

THANK YOU FOR YOUR FAVOR

Lord, open my eyes to the favor
You bestow on me each day
Let me stop and acknowledge
Each blessing you've sent my way

Let me pause and thank you
For your faithfulness to me
Unmerited care and protection
That comes solely from Thee

The things that I take for granted
Are mercies I failed to see
Help me to always remember
Your hand provided that for me

Because you love me always
You watch over me from above
I praise you for your lovingkindness
And cherish Your gifts of love

MATTHEW 6:19-21

"Do not store up for yourselves treasures on earth, where moth and rust destroy, and where thieves break in and steal. [20]But store up for yourselves treasures in heaven, where moth and rust do not destroy, and where thieves do not break in and steal. [21]For where your treasure is, there your heart will be also."

TREASURES

How do we measure success
In this world of "look at me"
A fancy house, a shiny new car
Clothes and shoes of designer quality

Working all day; playing all night
A rat race to "keep up with the Joneses"
The best vacations at 5-star hotels
Surely will disclose our importance

Where will this all get us in the end
When our earthly life is no more
The wealth and possessions so dear to us
Will not be ours anymore

We must remember the words of Jesus
Regarding the importance of you and me
Those that live by earth's success
In heaven will not be

The first will be last; the last will be first
A teaching to study and learn
Success in heaven's eyes
Is not what we temporally earn

We should store our treasures in heaven
Where our hearts should also be
For no one can serve two masters
You cannot serve both God and money

No other so deserving

of our worship and

praise

Our Savior forever

both now and always

MATTHEW 16:15-16

¹⁵*"But what about you?" he asked. "Who do you say I am?"*

¹⁶*Simon Peter answered, "You are the Christ, the Son of the living God."*

PHILIPPIANS 2:10, 11

¹⁰*that at the name of Jesus every knee should bow, in heaven and on earth and under the earth,*

¹¹*and every tongue confess that Jesus Christ is Lord, to the glory of God the Father.*

JESUS

Jesus is our salvation
The meaning of His name
Jesus means "Savior"
From sin that causes shame

Jesus is Christ
Anointed Messiah is He
Just the mention of His name
Will bring us to our knees

Jesus Christ, the Lamb of God
Worthy, worthy is He
He sacrificed Himself for us
On that shame-filled tree

Jesus Christ, the Son of God
Who reigns in heaven above
Blessing, honor and praise are due
For you deserve our love

Jesus, our returning King
We long for that sweet day
When all our sickness, toil and pain
Will be eternally washed away!

HEBREWS 9:15

For this reason Christ is the mediator of a new covenant, that those who are called may receive the promised eternal inheritance—now that he has died as a ransom to set them free from the sins committed under the first covenant.

GOD'S PLAN OF SALVATION

Awake, awake
My soul and sing
Praises to our risen King

Who came as a child
Born in Bethlehem
And grew to be
A teacher of men

He walked this earth
So we could be free
From the sins
That keep us from Calvary

He traveled the path
He was destined to take
And endured trials
For mankind's sake

From the riches of heaven
To a carpenter's son
We were his purpose
God's salvation for everyone

How awesome and amazing
This plan set in place
A new covenant from God
Full of mercy and grace

No other so deserving
Of worship and praise
Our Savior forever
Both now and always

MATTHEW 7:21-23

"Not everyone who says to me, 'Lord, Lord,' will enter the kingdom of heaven, but only he who does the will of my Father who is in heaven. ²²Many will say to me on that day, 'Lord, Lord, did we not prophesy in your name, and in your name drive out demons and perform many miracles?' ²³Then I will tell them plainly, 'I never knew you. Away from me, you evildoers!'"

DON'T CALL YOURSELF A CHRISTIAN

Don't call yourself a Christian
If you don't walk the walk
Going to church never cuts it
Words spoken; just senseless talk

Don't call yourself a Christian
While using it to state a cause
That completely ignores Christ's mission
While you look for the world's applause

To be a Christian means Christ-like
Not just a proper noun
When you say it please be mindful
It represents the Savior's crown

Jesus died to forgive us
He suffered for you and me
As the means for our salvation
From sin to set us free

So, if you want to be a Christian
Accept Christ in your heart
The change will be remarkable
Your life will reflect the new start

Call yourself a Christian
When you daily walk the way
Shone to us in God's precious word
And His word you long to obey

It's not a perfect journey
There are trials, stumbles and falls
Yet, Christ will forgive and be there
When on His name you call

So truly become that Christian
That your words expressed and claimed
For nothing brings joy to heaven
Then a lost soul Christ now gained

MATTHEW 16:24, 25

24Then Jesus said to his disciples, "If anyone would come after me, he must deny himself and take up his cross and follow me. 25For whoever wants to save his life will lose it, but whoever loses his life for me will find it."

WHAT WOULD I HAVE DONE

What would I have done
If I lived when Jesus came
Would I have called Him Master
Or joined the crowd's disdain

Would I have seen a Savior
Who came to die for me?
Or would I have scoffed and laughed
As He carried that cross-shaped tree

Would I have cried, "Crucify!"
"He must be put to death!"
Or would I have wept at the cross
Watching His last breath

My hope is that I would have been
Just as I am today
A follower of the one who came
To take my sins away

MATTHEW 1:21

"She will give birth to a son, and you are to give him the name
Jesus, because he will save his people from their sins."

I PETER 2:24

He himself bore our sins in his body on the tree, so that we
might die to sins and live for righteousness; by his wounds you
have been healed.

TWO TREES

When asked about our favorite day
That we love best of all
Most respond, without a doubt
It's Christmas Day by far

What a marvelous time that we enjoy
Of family, food and cheer
The world sings out carols
That are sung from year to year

We celebrate our Savior's birth
How giving He must be
The birthday gifts He should receive
Are underneath our tree

The most unselfish gift of all
Was born that special day
Our Savior came in human form
To take our sins away

May Christmas always be treasured
As a reminder to you and me
That Jesus was born on that day
To die upon a tree

Not a tree with ornaments
Tinsel, lights or stars
But one that became a cross
Where He died for sins that were ours

Two trees to remind us
Of two miraculous days
One to celebrate His birth
The second took our sins away

JAMES 4:7

Submit yourselves, then, to God. Resist the devil, and he will flee from you.

ISAIAH 43:25

"I, even I, am he who blots out your transgressions, for my own sake, and remembers your sins not more."

YOU WON'T BE FORGIVEN

When we do wrong
And lose our way
It's troubling how Satan
Has a lot to say

Before we gave in
To that sinful misstep
He whispered that God
"Would forgive and forget"

When we realize the error
In what we have done
And admit it was not acceptable
To our Master's Son

Satan keeps telling us
Quite loud and clear,
"God will never forgive you,"
He reverbs in our ear

These lies are not true
Just a trick and a scheme
Bow your head and ask
For the forgiveness you need

Be strong and take heart
God quickly forgives
Then it's erased from His memory
That's a promise He gives

Quit falling for ploys
That lead to deceit
Seek the truth from God's Word
And Satan you'll defeat!

He answers according

to His will

We must trust His reply

PSALM 46:10

"Be still and know that I am God;
I will be exalted among the nations,
I will be exalted in the earth."

JEREMIAH 33:3

'Call to me and I will answer you and tell you great and unsearchable things you do not know'

DOES GOD HEAR US

How do we know
That God hears us
A question often pondered
Does He speak audibly
All have often wondered

Is He really out there
Listening when we call?
Are we wasting our time
Praying to Him at all?

The best response
To this thought
Is found in God's own Word
Faith and hope are a must
To believe we have been heard

"Be still and know that I AM GOD"
Informs what we should do
Sit and pray; stop and listen
It will be revealed to you

It's amazing how a tiny thought
Comes just when it is needed
An answer so remarkable
You know God interceded

Does God hear?
Does God answer?
On this we can rely
He answers according to HIS will
We must trust His reply

JAMES 1:12

Blessed is the man who perseveres under trial, because when he has stood the test, he will receive the crown of life that GOD promised to those who love him.

TRIALS ARE ALLOWED BY GOD

If trials never came our way
Would we soon become complacent?
Why would we need God above
When life is fine and decent

If all our skies were blue
And our clouds were never grey
Would we need our Master?
Or go on our merry way

If all our bills were paid
And all our wants were met
The employment ladder was at the top
And we smugly sat content

Would we take the time
To bow our head and pray?
Thank God for His blessings
Or request His will that day?

Take this time to ponder
The basic questions here
It's quite obvious to see
God wants us ever near

Trials are allowed by Him
To draw us to His throne
So, when He knows the time is right
His perfect will He'll make known

PHILIPPIANS 4:6, 7

[6]Do not be anxious about anything, but in everything, by prayer and petition, with thanksgiving, present your requests to God. [7]And the peace of God, which transcends all understanding, will guard your hearts and your minds in Christ Jesus.

WHISPER, "I'LL SEE YOU THROUGH"

Some days my heart just longs
For quiet without cares
I yearn for peace and happiness;
Life without despair

I know the way, the truth, the life
I know what I should do
Yet, that human element steps in
And tries to pull me away from you

I want that song in the night
That you have promised to me
I must release these burdens
At Your feet so that I'll be free

You give me my daily bread
You forgive, my sin; my shame
My needs you meet day by day
I should have no reason to complain

How I permit my thoughts and griefs
To muddle up my day
Is not at all what you expect
You don't want me lead astray

Guide me back when I allow
My thoughts to steer from You
When I feel empty and alone
Whisper, "I'll see you through"

I pray that my lips

will speak that which

honors You

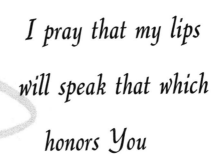

COLOSSIANS 4:6

Let your conversation be always full of grace, seasoned with salt, so that you may know how to answer everyone.

CONVERSATIONS

What is my conversation
When I talk with friends each day
Is it gossip? Is it shopping?
Is God pleased with what I say?

Is it filled with truth and happiness
Did I speak one word of You?
Did I reflect Your image
When I voiced my view

Was I kind and tenderhearted
Were my answers thoughtfully said
Did my mouth speak Your heart
Or mindless words instead

I pray that my lips
Will speak that which honors You
Words of wisdom and compassion
As Your Word instructs me to

May my friends hear You
In all I have to say
Because, what You expect from me
Is what I strive for day by day

I dedicate the following poem in memory of my
Father, Pete Sanitate.
I was blessed with a Godly father
whose words of wisdom were more
valuable than silver or gold.

His prayers surrounded me 24/7...
He is sorely missed.

My Father Remembered

The day you left your earthly home
And went to live in heaven
Broke my heart and pierced my soul
Would this pain ever lessen?

The times we shared year after year
Together through laughter or pain
In an instant became just memories
Sweet thoughts are what remain

A Godly leader by example
The Word of God you revered
You lived by those principles daily
And from those standards you never veered

Your prayers "hedged" our family in
To God's safety and care
Your daily time before God's throne
Was a blessing beyond compare

Holidays, birthdays, and family events
Still occur as time goes by
That place where you always sat...
Can still bring a tear to my eye

I'm thankful for the years that I had
A tear here or there's a good thing
It just means you were adored and admired
And as my Father you were amazing!